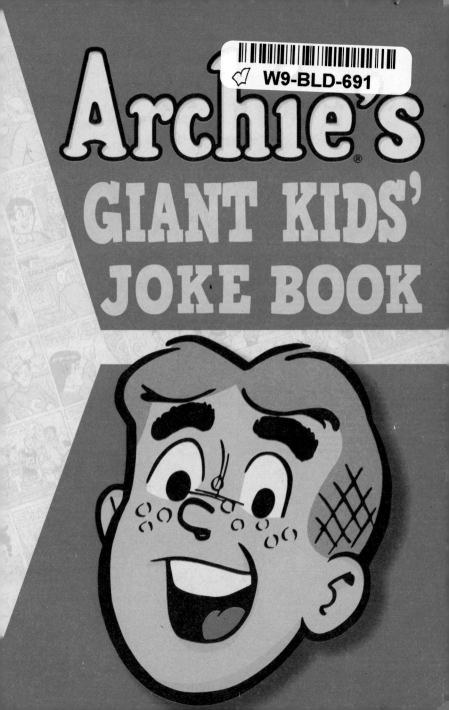

Archie's
GIANT KIDS'
JOKE BOOK

Archie's
GIANT KIDS' JOKE BOOK

Published by Archie Comic Publications, Inc.
325 Fayette Avenue, Mamaroneck, New York 10543-2318.

ArchieComics.com
ISBN: 978-1-936975-28-0

Publisher / Co-CEO: Jon Goldwater
Co-CEO: Nancy Silberkleit
President: Mike Pellerito
Co-President / Editor-In-Chief: Victor Gorelick
Senior Vice President - Sales / Business Development: Jim Sokolowski
Senior Vice President - Publishing / Operations: Harold Buchholz
Executive Director of Editorial: Paul Kaminski
Project Coordinator & Book Design: Joe Morciglio
Production Manager: Stephen Oswald
Lead Production Artist: Carlos Antunes
Proofreader / Editorial Assistant: Jamie Lee Rotante
Production: Steven Golebiewski, Rosario "Tito" Peña, Kari Silbergleit, Pat Woodruff
Production Intern: Mike Crowe

Archie's

GIANT KIDS' JOKE BOOK

LAUGHS AND GAGS BY:

BOB MONTANA, FRANK DOYLE,
BILL VIGODA, GEORGE GLADIR,
AL HARTLEY, BILL GOLLIHER,
HY EISMAN, DICK MALMGREN,
MIKE PELLOWSKI, VIC BLOOM,
HARRY LUCEY, GEORGE FRESE,
BOB BOLLING, SAMM SCHWARTZ,
STAN GOLDBERG, REX LINDSEY,
DAN DECARLO JR., JEFF SHULTZ,
JOE EDWARDS, RUDY LAPICK,
TERRY AUSTIN, BARRY GROSSMAN,
ROD OLLERENSHAW, BOB SMITH
JON D'AGOSTINO, BILL YOSHIDA,
JACK MORELLI, AND DAN DECARLO

YOU DID IT!

You've just picked up the ultimate book of funny panels, crazy cartoons, wacky jokes and terrible puns! If you didn't actually buy it, go and bug your parents until they do!

You'll find all sorts of crazy stuff in this book. From sports gags and food puns to wacky one-liners and riddles, the jokes just keep on coming!

So, what are you waiting for?

Go on! Get reading! GO!

Q: Why did the
   Easter egg hide?

A: Because it was a
   little chicken!

IF YOU'RE READING THIS TURN THE PAGE!!

A: Because if it flew over the bay it would be called a bagel!

Q: How do you communicate with a fish?

Sharks do not chew their food, they swallow it whole.

Q: Why is a swordfish's nose 11 inches long?

A: If it was 12 inches, it would be a "foot"!

Jughead also does not chew his food.

A: You drop it a line!

Q: Where did the dermatologist start his business?

A: From scratch!

Q: Why did the
bacon laugh?

A: Because the egg
cracked a yolk!

Q: What do you call a cow with no legs?

A: Ground Beef!

Q: What is smarter than a talking bird?

A: A spelling bee!

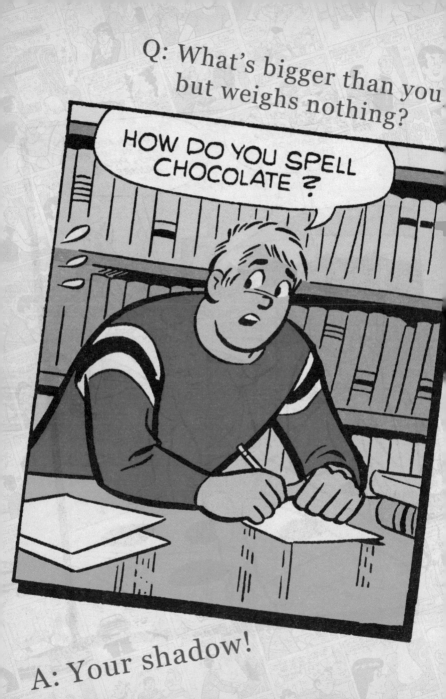

Q: When does Friday come before Thursday?

Q: When is a door a jar?

A: When it's open!

A: In the dictionary!

Q: What goes up but never comes down?

A: Your age!

Even Mr. Weatherbee thinks these jokes are awful!

Q: What gets wetter when it dries?

A: A towel!

Q: What kind of bird likes to make fun of people?

A: A Mock-ing bird

Q: What do you call an alligator who lies?

A: A Croc-odile!

Q: What do you call a deer with no eyes?

Q: What bird is always sad?

A: I have no I-Deer!!

You can relax now!
The jokes are almost over!

A: A blue jay!

Why did the boy throw the alarm clock out the window?

It wouldn't stop ringing!
...ou didn't think he wanted to
...ee time fly did you?

IF YOU CAN READ THIS YOU HAVE AN
AMAZING TALENT FOR READING BACKWARDS.
IT'S A USELESS TALENT BUT A TALENT NONETHELESS!

Did he just kiss a dog?

Q: :What did the digital clock say to the grandfather clock?

A: Look grandpa, no hands!

That's "ruff"!

A: Sue!

Q: Who is not hungry after Thanksgiving?

Q: What time is it when you're being chased by ten elephants?

A: 10 after 1!

A: The turkey! He's already stuffed!

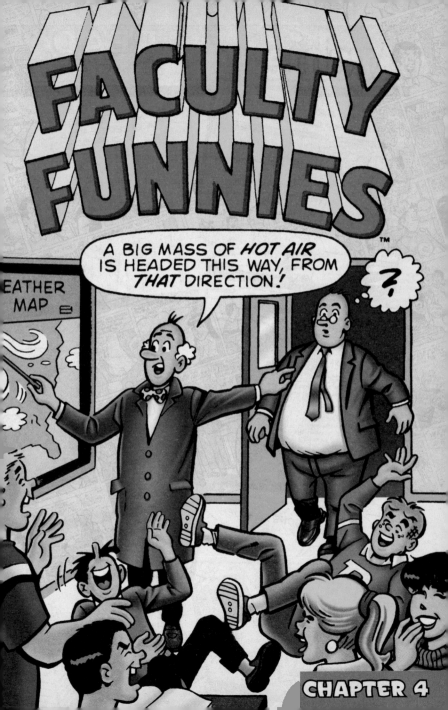

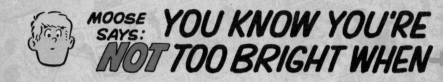

HUMPTY DUMPTY IS YOUR IDEA OF A TRAGIC LITERARY CHARACTER!

MOTHER GOOSE

MOOSE SAYS: **YOU KNOW YOU'RE _NOT_ TOO BRIGHT WHEN···**

TEACHER MARKS YOUR TEST PAPER 'ZERO' BEFORE SHE READS IT!

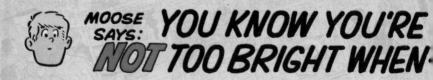

MOOSE SAYS: **YOU KNOW YOU'RE NOT TOO BRIGHT WHEN·**

CHAPTER 5

Q: What do you call an annoying giraffe?

A: A pain in the neck!

SUMMER JOBS

HERE'S THE JOB REGGIE WANTED...

...HERE'S THE JOB HE GOT!

Q: What's the best time
to go to the dentist

A: Tooth-hurty!

Q: What do you call a fish with no eye?

A: Fshhh!

Q: What did one toilet say to the other?

A: You look flushed!

Q: What did the pony say when it had a sore throat?

A: I apologize, I'm a little horse!

"WORK QUIRK"

DAD AND I HAVE THIS GREAT NEW PART-TIME BUSINESS!

ANDREWS AN

...WE HELP CART AWAY JUNK AND CLUTTER FOR A FEE...

WE GET EXERCISE, AND THE MONEY IS **REAL GOOD!**

AND YOU PROVIDE A MUCH NEEDED SERVICE!

BUT MOM INSISTS THAT WE GIVE UP THE BUSINESS...

HOW COME?

DAD AND I CAN'T RESIST BRINGING HOME SOME OF THE STUFF OURSELVES!

AND

END

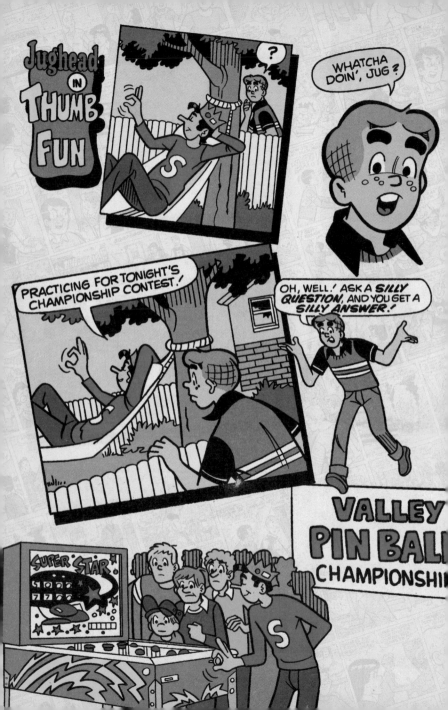

Q: Who has the easiest job in the world??

A: Candlemakers! They only work on wick-ends!

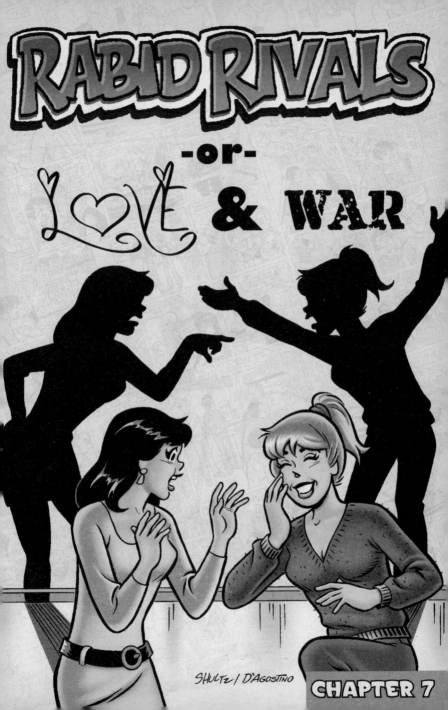

Q: What's black and white and makes a lot of noise?

A: A zebra with a drum kit.

Q: What do you call a blind dinosaur?

A: A do-you-think-he-saur-us!

"Doga" is a type of yoga in which people use yoga to achieve harmony with their pets. Dogs can either be used as props for their owners or they can do the stretches themselves.

Q: What is the most musical fish?

A: A Tune-a-fish!

T TO KNOW THE ORIGINAL JOKES?
OUT AT WWW.ARCHIECOMICS.COM/JOKE

SLOSH

Q: Why should you never fall in love
   with a tennis player?

Steffi Graf and Andre Agassi
were the first married couple
to have won both the men's and
women's singles Wimbledon Championships.

A: Because to them,
"love" means nothing!